101 Am
Do in Norway

Introduction

So you're going to Norway, huh? You lucky lucky thing! You are sure in for a treat because Norway is, without a doubt, one of the most special travel destinations on the face of the planet – and so criminally underrated. It offers something for every visitor, so whether you are into exploring the local gastronomic scene, buying some special items of Norwegian design, or even dog sledding, Norway has something that you'll treasure.

This guide will take you on a journey from the major cities like Oslo, Trondheim, Bergen, Tromso, and the islands as well

In this guide, we'll be giving you the low down on:
- the very best things to shove in your pie hole, whether you need to want to chow down on some local brown cheese or enjoy a 3 Michelin star fine dining experience
- incredible festivals, from electronic festivals with world famous headliners through to the festivals celebrating Norwegian indigenous culture

- the coolest historical and cultural sights that you simply cannot afford to miss like Norwegian art fairs, and ancient fortresses and castles
- the most incredible outdoor adventures, whether you want a Snowmobile Safari experience, or you'd like to try salmon fishing in a fjord
- where to shop for authentic souvenirs so that you can remember your trip to Norway forever
- the places where you can party like a local and make new friends
- and tonnes more coolness besides!

Let's not waste any more time – here are the 101 most amazing, spectacular, and cool things not to miss in Norway!

1. Stroll Through the Sculptures in Ekebergparken

Norway is a country that is full of nature, and even in the capital city, Oslo, you are never far away from some green space or an expanse of water. We are particularly fond of Ekebergparken because it's a park that combines the very best of nature and culture thanks to its impressive sculpture garden. There are many sculptures from artists all over the world, and in a city than can be somewhat pricey, this activity is 100% free.

(Kongsveien 23, 0193 Oslo; https://ekebergparken.com)

2. Look for Whales off the Coast of Andenes

One of the most magical experiences that you can have in Norway is whale watching off the coast. Probably the best spot for this is the village of Andenes, which you will find right at the northern tip of the country. The best time to see the whales is from December until March, right in the dead of winter, but if you are there in summer there is still a chance of seeing a good amount of sperm whales. You'll be taken on a boat off the coast so you have the best chance of seeing whales up close.

3. Tuck Into New Nordic Cuisine at Oslo's Brutus

When in an exciting capital city like Oslo, it's important to eat in at least one really good restaurant. We know that Oslo can be expensive, but we promise that your experience at Brutus will be worth every penny. The style of both the food and décor here is earthy and unpretentious, a lot like Norway itself. Using ingredients such as brown cheese, wild wood sorrel, and Norwegian capers, this is an authentic taste of the country, and their natural wine list makes the whole experience even more delightful.

(Eiriks gate 2, 0650 Oslo; http://barbrutus.no)

4. Camp at Tvindefossen Waterfall

If you are somebody who loves the great outdoors, Norway is not simply a place that offers wonderful landscapes, but it also provides the opportunity to truly immerse yourself in the spectacular scenery the country has to offer. Seeing a beautiful a waterfall is one thing, but at Tvindefossen waterfall you actually have the chance to camp there as well. Waking up in the fresh Norwegian air and taking your morning shower in this waterfall is an invigorating experience you won't want to miss.

5. Get to Grips With Norwegian Art at Nasjonalgalleriet

There's a number of really wonderful museums and galleries in Norway, but the Nasjonalgalleriet, or National Museum of Art, Architecture, and Design, might be the most impressive of the whole lot. Founded all the way back in 1837, this museum has the largest collection of Norwegian art to be found anywhere. You could easily spend a couple of days here if you're a real art lover, and the most famous piece of art on display is Munch's 'The Scream'.

(Universitetsgata 13, 0164 Oslo; www.nasjonalmuseet.no)

6. Enjoy a Hearty Seafood Meal at Fiskeriet

With so much water around Norway, this is one country when you can be assured of a fantastic seafood dinner, and if it's fish and seafood that really does it for you, be sure to chow down at Fiskeriet in Oslo. Actually, this is more of a seafood store, that has a small kitchen and dining area, making it all the more intimate and special. The menu is small and simple, but everything tastes great. Think traditional fish and chips, fresh oysters, and fish soup.

(Youngstorget 2b, 0181 Oslo; www.fiskeriet.net)

7. Purchase Local Handicrafts at the Villvin Market

When you travel around Norway, you will no doubt want to bring home some things that can remind you of this fascinating and very special country forever. If you happen to be in the country during July, try to make it to the Villvin market in Risor, which has to be the number one handicrafts fair anywhere in Norway. You can pick up cool textiles, glassware, ceramics, paper-wares, woodwork, leather goods, and so much more, and all from independent makers and designers.

(http://villvin.no/smile/marked)

8. Get Close to the Animals at Nammskogan Familiepark

If you are travelling with kids, a trip to a nature park with impressive wildlife is always a wonderful idea. Trones, a village in the central part of the country, is home to one of Norway's best nature parks, Nammskogan Familiepark. Walk around the park and you and the little ones will be able to get close to more than 30 species of animals and birds. With wolverines, wolves, bears, and lynxes, there are plenty of winter creatures to get to know.

(Tronesfjellveien 534, 7892 Trones; https://familieparken.no)

9. Sip on Decadent Cocktails at Torggata Botaniske

If you're in Oslo on a Friday night, you might get a hankering for a strong cocktail (or three), and when that desire strikes, Torggata Botaniske is the number one place to go. As the name suggests, this bar has a botanical theme with lots of floral and natural flavours (not to mention the ivy covering the walls). With ingredients such as rosemary syrup, angostura bitters, peychaud bitters, and pear liqueur, it's the place to have something a little out of the ordinary.

(Torggata 17B, 0183 Oslo)

10. View the Northern Lights in Tromso

One of the most iconic experiences that Norway has to offer is the Northern Lights, and it's with good reason. One of the best places to view the Northern Lights is in Tromso. The very basic idea of the Northern Lights is that charged particles emit an incredible array of lights into the atmosphere. Describing it is one thing, but it truly has to be seen to be believed. You have most chance of seeing the lights in Tromso from early September to early April.

11. Hike Around Reinebringen

Norway is not a destination that you would think of as being particularly mountainous and to offer great mountain hiking, but seek and you shall find. Reinebringen is far from being one of the tallest mountains in Norway, but the hike to the top is one of the most challenging with many steep and slippery sections. With that said, the view from the lookout point is worth all the effort. Just please be sure to wear very sturdy hiking boots.

12. Take in a Show at the Oslo Opera House

When you think of opera houses, you no doubt think of grand old, opulent buildings. The Oslo Opera House is something altogether very different because it only opened fairly recently in 2008, but the performances staged there are still very much world class. If you only have limited time, a walk across the roof of the building is a must, but if you're really an arts lover then be sure to check their programme ahead of time and book tickets for one of their opera or ballet performances.

(Kirsten Flagstads Plass 1, 0150 Oslo; https://operaen.no)

13. Browse Through the Books at Cappelens Forslag

If you are overwhelmed by modern technology and you long for the days of analogue, be sure to pay a visit to Cappelens Forslag, an independent bookshop in Oslo with a selection of new, used, and antiquarian books that will get any bookworm salivating. You will find some really cool cult literature and out of print books here that you just won't find in other places. Plus, there is a selection of photographs, vinyl and prints to peruse.

(Bernt Ankers gate 4B, 0183 Oslo; www.cappelensforslag.no)

14. Visit a Typical Farm of Western Norway

Even though Norway is a country with extreme weather (well, only on the cold side), agriculture is still extremely important to the country, and it can be a lovely idea to actually visit a farm so you can get to grips with rural life in Norway first hand. Syse Gard in western Norway would be a great choice. On the farm you can witness a sheep farm, orchards, and you can take back some delicious goodies from the farm shop. The chutneys and smoked mutton are especially good.

(Apalvegen 104, 5730 Ulvik; https://sysegard.no)

15. Get Close to Viking Ships at Vikingskiphuset

One of the most famous things about Norway and Scandinavia more broadly is the glory of its Viking Age and the splendour of its majestic Viking ships. You can take in all this majesty first hand at the impressive Vikingskipuset, or Viking Ship Museum, in Oslo. This museum is worth a visit if only for the complete Oseberg Ship, which was rescued from the largest ship burial known in world history. If you happen to be travelling with kids, this is a place they'll be fascinated by.

(Huk Aveny 35, 0287 Oslo; www.khm.uio.no/besok-oss/vikingskipshuset)

16. Go Salmon Fishing in the Romsdalsfjord

If your idea of the perfect getaway involves being close to a vast expanse of water so you can go fishing to your heart's content, there are many wonderful fishing options for you in Norway. Romsdalsfjord is one of the longest fjords in Norway, and is celebrated for its incredible salmon fishing. It is a good idea to organise a trip with a local company who can take you deep into the fjord because that's where you'll get the biggest catches.

17. Discover the World of Edvard Munch at Munchmuseet

You might not think of Norway as one of the art capitals of the world, but it has a long artistic tradition, and if you have never heard of another Norwegian artist, you have almost certainly heard of Edvard Munch. Munchmuseet, or Munch Museum is the number one place in the world to get to grips with the great artist, his life, and works. Over half of all the artist's works are here, including 1200 paintings and 18,000 prints.

(Tøyengata 53, 0578 Oslo; https://munchmuseet.no)

18. Enjoy a Gorgeous Sauna Experience at SALT

Your holiday time should be full of moments when you truly allow yourself to relax and allow the responsibilities of daily life to slide from your shoulders. And what better way to unwind than with a gorgeous sauna experience? In Oslo, our favourite spot for this is SALT, because it's way more than just a sauna. You'll be sharing the space with up to 120 other people, and there is always a programme of live entertainment with live music, dance, and theatre to make your visit extra special.

(Langkaia 1, 0150 Oslo; www.salted.no)

19. Eat Brown Cheese at Breakfast Time

Okay so Norwegian food might not be celebrated right across the world, but this is certainly not to say that there are not plenty of delicious things to chow down on in the country. At breakfast time, something you should definitely try to eat is the local brown cheese, or brunost. Unbelievably, some of this cheese has been discovered in a pot dating to 650 BC, so it represents something deeply historical in Norway. The cheese has whey added to the mix, and it has a soft texture with a sweeter taste than most cheeses.

20. Relax on Stunning Ramberg Beach

Although the beaches of Norway are not famous around the globe, once you step foot on Ramberg Beach, you will start to seriously question why Norway isn't more firmly set on the map as a beach destination. Ramberg is actually one of Norway's islands. Yes, it's more effort to get there, but it is well worth it. The sand is so white and the sea is so blue that you might just think you are in the Caribbean rather than northernmost Europe for a moment.

21. Take to the Slopes for the Oslo Ski Festival

Norway is famed the world over for its spectacular skiing conditions, and if you love nothing more than to take to the slopes and immerse yourself in ski culture, the Holmenkollen Ski Festival in Oslo is a must visit. It takes place in March each year, and has been running annually since 1892. The festival is packed with exciting competitions including ski jumping and cross country skiing for both men and women. There's also plenty of kids' activities if you happen to be travelling with little adventurers.

(https://holmenkollenskifestival.no)

22. Hike Along the Svartfjell Trail

If you love nothing more than to strap on your hiking boots and feel the fresh air fill your lungs, there are so many great hiking trails for you to choose from throughout Norway. On the Svartfjell Trail, the hike lasts for 12km and begins at Spidsbergseter in the middle of the country. This is not a particularly difficult hike, so just a basic fitness level should suffice. You'll walk around the mountains and see a gorgeous lake.

23. Rock Out at the Annual Oya Festival

When you think of festival destinations around the world, Norway probably wouldn't be the first country that springs to mind, but the Norwegians party with the best of them at Oya Festival, which takes place annually in August when the summer days last way into the night. This is a festival primarily for rock lovers so if you love live instruments and jamming out, this is the ticket for you. Previous performers have included Arctic Monkeys, Morrissey, and Beck.

(https://oyafestivalen.no/en)

24. Stroll Through the Frognerparken

While Oslo can't be said to have a huge amount of hustle and bustle, there are times when you might want to see no cars at all and just relax and unwind in green serenity. When that moment strikes, you should venture to Frognerparken, the largest of the city's many parks. The park contains over 14,000 plants from more than 150 different plant species, and it has the largest rose collection in all of Norway, so it's a perfect place for a nature lover to take a stroll.

(Kirkeveien, 0268 Oslo)

25. Take in a Play at the Nationaltheatret

Dating all the way back to 1899, Oslo's Nationaltheatret, or National Theatre, is not just a great place to see a play, but also an important part of the city's history. Ibsen is probably the most famous playwright to ever have emerged from Norway, and this theatre is considered the home of Ibsen's plays where you can still see many Ibsen performances to this day. If you are a real Ibsen fanatic then be sure to check out the biennial International Ibsen Festival that is held here.

(Johanne Dybwads plass 1, 0161 Oslo; www.nationaltheatret.no)

26. Walk Across the Futuristic Skywalk, Aurland Lookout

Norway is a country with no shortage of breath taking views, and one of the most spectacular of the lot is the Aurland Lookout in the Sognefjord area. This skywalk really does take you into the skies, as it is located around 2000 feet above the ground. The skywalk will take you through the treetops and then dramatically plunges southwards so that it appears that people are walking off the edge. Those who are scared of heights could find it a touch too scary.

27. Relax Around Sognsvann Lake

One of the best things about jetting off for a holiday is getting away from it all, and allowing all the stresses and responsibilities of life to melt away. And where better to relax than around a perfectly peaceful lake? If that sounds good to you, we would love to recommend Sognsvann Lake that lies just north of Oslo, making it perfect for a city break getaway. It's perfect for walking and running,

the water is safe for swimming, and you can even bring a
fishing rod and try to catch dinner.

28. Indulge a History Buff at the Historisk Museum

Whether you know a little or a lot about Norwegian
history, the Historisk Museum is sure to be enlightening
and entertaining, and a great place to spend a few hours if
the skies are looking grey. There are many collections
inside the museum, and we especially enjoy the artefacts
from the Viking Age. You will find jewellery, ornaments,
coins, and even the only complete Viking helmet that has
ever been found.

*(Frederiks gate 2, 0164 Oslo; www.khm.uio.no/besok-
oss/historisk-museum)*

29. Stroll Through the Tjuvholmen Sculpture Park

In an expensive city like Oslo, it's rather nice to find
things to do that are completely free, and actually there's a
surprising amount of free activities. Taking a stroll
through beautiful Tjuvholmen Sculpture Park won't cost
you a penny, and it's one of our favourite sunny day
activities. There are seven sculptures in the park, all

designed by contemporary artists that have different styles. We love how the contemporary design merges with the nature all around.

(Strandpromenaden 2, 0252 Oslo; http://tjuvholmen.no)

30. Fill Your Belly at Oslo's Mathallen

If you're a foodie traveller, Oslo might not be right at the top of your must-visit destination list, but you'll think otherwise once you have spent some time in the capital city. If you'd like to sample a little bit of everything in a casual setting, make your way to Mathallen, the city's premiere food court. You'll find a great mix of local and international food, so go in hungry and feast on the likes of French pastries, German sausages, pickled fish from Norway, and wash it all down with plenty of Champagne.

(Vulkan 5, 0178 Oslo; https://mathallenoslo.no)

31. Drive Across the Atlantic Ocean Road

Norway is actually a rather expansive country, and the landscapes can change dramatically as you travel from place to place. For this reason, renting a car can be a really great idea. You can take in these landscapes as you whizz along the roads, and take your time doing it. The Atlantic Ocean Road is a particularly spectacular route. You will actually be driving over water as this road connects the mainland to several islands, and it has even been voted the World's Most Beautiful Drive.

32. Step Back in Time at Hovag's Viking Market

The village of Hovag is a small, quaint place in the south of the country that you probably wouldn't visit as it's not listed in most guides. But history lovers should definitely make it there for their very charming Viking market, which typically takes place in the beginning of July. You will see traditional Viking crafts being brought to life, and actually see goodies being made in front of your eyes. Even if you know nothing about Viking activities, this market is a fascinating and enjoyable visit.

33. Take a Snowmobile Safari Through Svalbard Island

If you really wish to explore the Arctic, and can't get enough of the beautiful frosty landscapes, you should make your way to the Svalbard Islands. This is a really magical, isolated part of the world like nowhere else you can imagine. Get lucky and you can kayak between icebergs and even witness polar bears. But it's so cold and barren here that it's impossible to wander around. A much better idea is to get yourself on a snowmobile safari and explore the islands in style!

34. Enjoy a Swim in Oslo's Toyenbadet

Travelling to new far flung places is very exciting but it can also be exhausting, and sometimes you might just want to relax by the side of a pool and swim a few laps. Fortunately, there's quite a few public pools in Oslo, and Toyenbadet is the best of the bunch. In fact, this is not just one pool, but a whole assortment. There are two indoor pools for the winter months, and two outdoor months for when the sun is shining down on Oslo.

(Helgesens gate 90, 0550 Oslo)

35. Learn About Sami Culture at the Riddu Riddu Festival

There are so many different highlights to a trip to Norway, from the landscapes to the food, but don't forget to absorb as much local culture as you can as well. A great place to do this is at the annual Riddu Riddu Festival in July, which celebrates Sami music and culture. The Sami are an indigenous culture of the north, and this wonderful festival makes these little known people visible for a world that chooses to ignore them. Fascinating.

(http://riddu.no/en)

36. Take the Scenic Oslo to Trondheim Train

You might be tempted to take a short flight from Oslo in the south to Trondheim in the north, but we think that taking the train is a much better option. Yes, the journey is 7 hours long, but you get to see the most spectacular scenery along the way, and this journey isn't just a way to get from one city to another, it's a legitimate experience. As you chug along, you will pass through the Gudbrandsdalen Valley and the Dovrefjell mountain range.

37. Have Fun at the Ice Music Festival in Geilo

Geilo is a gorgeous town in the south of Norway that is well known for its ski trails and beautiful mountain resorts, but what sets it apart for us is the annual Ice Music Festival that takes place there. We're not just talking live bands performing against an icy landscape. In fact, all the instruments are carved from ice! All the instruments are played outside in sub-zero temperatures, so there is no chance of a meltdown. The festival is held in February each year.

(www.icemusicfestivalnorway.no)

38. Stroll Through the Tromso Arctic-Alpine Botanical Garden

Nature lovers might think there is more than enough to explore in the wild so that it's actually unnecessary to visit a botanical garden, but as soon as you step through the doors of the Tromso Arctic-Alpine Botanical Garden you will not regret your visit. There is something beautiful to see no matter what time of year you visit. There are 25 separate gardens, and you can even find African plants that survive the Norwegian winter. It's free to enter, so no excuses.

(Stakkevollvegen 200, 9019 Tromso;
https://uit.no/tmu/botanisk)

39. Get a Little Tipsy at the Stavanger Wine Festival

Travelling around Europe is great for many things, and the wine is certainly one of the highlights, but Norway probably isn't a country that you intend to visit with the intention of trying new and exciting wines. But that's exactly what you'll get at the Stavanger Wine Festival, hosted in the charming southwestern city of Stavanger. Twelve local restaurants club together to put together this festival, and invite some of the best wine producers from around Europe to showcase their wares. It takes place in March each year.

40. Take the Ferry to Hovedoya Island

Who would have thought that you can take a ferry ride from the capital city of Oslo and visit an isolated island with incredible nature? Well, you can. The ferry ride to Hovedoya island takes just minutes, and once you are there you will be immersed in a completely different world. There are two beaches on the island, which are perfect for sunny days, and there are also some designated barbecue spots by the beach where you can grill to your heart's content.

41. Take in a View of Bergen From Mount Floyen

If you make it to the city of Bergen (which you should), be sure to find your way to Mount Floyen, which reaches 399 metres above sea level, and is one of the city's main attractions. If you are worried about climbing your way to the top, fear not because there is a funicular railway that will take you to the peak in just six short minutes. From the peak, you have a stunning view of Bergen, its seaward approaches, and the beautiful fjords that surround the city.

42. Try a Traditional Dish: Lutefisk

One of the greatest things about travelling to Norway is that you will have the chance to try lots of foods you have never tried before. You might think about travelling to Italy before Norway, but you've probably already tried every kind of pasta and pizza under the sun. But it's unlikely that you have tried the popular Norwegian dish, Lutefisk. White fish is air dried and then soaked in water and lye. This reduces the protein content and gives it a gelatinous texture.

43. Walk Across the Geiranger Skywalk

If you are not afraid of heights and you want to take in one of the most epic views in all of Norway, be sure to check out the Geiranger Skywalk, which is actually Europe's highest fjord view from a road. The viewpoint takes you to an astonishing height of 1500 metres above sea level, and you will have an awe-inspiring view of the fjords and the snow covered mountains all while taking in big gulps of fresh mountain air.

(www.dalsnibba.no)

44. Take in the Majesty of the Arctic Cathedral

When you think of cathedrals, you no doubt think about tall, historic structures with towering spires and stained glass windows, but the Arctic Cathedral in Tromso is something altogether very different. This concrete metal and concrete church was only built in 1965, and has angular design features that make it look somewhat similar to the Sydney Opera House. The church has incredible acoustics so do check out one of the many church concerts if you have the opportunity.

(www.ishavskatedralen.no)

45. Go Back in Time at Akershus Castle

If you are a big-time history buff and you like visiting castles, you might be more inclined to visit the UK or Spain, which are bursting to the seams with castles, but Norway has a few impressive castles too, and we really love Akershus Castle. This medieval castle has a history that extends all the way back to the 13th century, and has experienced many renovations and additions since then. The banquet halls, Royal Mausoleum, and government reception rooms are very impressive.

(www.forsvarsbygg.no/no/festningene/finn-din-festning/akershus-festning/english)

46. Go Dog Sledding in the Lyngen Alps

One of the wonderful things about travelling to Norway is that you can be exposed to all kinds of winter activities that you might have never even thought about trying before. For example, how does dog sledding take your fancy? This is an activity that the whole family can enjoy, and the Lyngen Alps is the place to do it. Alaskan Huskies

pull groups of 2-6 people along in the pure white snow –
something to remember forever.

47. Keep Kids Entertained at the Norwegian Museum of Science & Technology

Travelling with kids is a great experience, but you also
have to make sure they are entertained at all times. If the
day is a bit cloudy and you can't do any outdoor activities,
the Norwegian Museum of Science & Technology in Oslo
is a fantastic idea. This is the place to indulge all of your
curiosities. You and your kids will have the chance to build
cars and run them on a racetrack, work with 3D printers
and laser cutters, create your own magnificent inventions,
and much more.

(Kjelsåsveien 143, 0491 Oslo; www.tekniskmuseum.no)

48. Get Artsy at the Lillehammer Art Museum

If you want to visit an art museum while in Norway, you
will definitely have the most opportunity in Oslo, but if
you find yourself in Lillehammer, the Lillehammer Art
Museum is a definite must-visit. Although not in the
capital city, you'll find over 1500 works of art there

making it more than possible to spend a very full afternoon wandering around the aisles. You can see Norwegian visual art from 1830 to the present day, as well as a significant number of international works.

(Stortorget 2, 2609 Lillehammer;
https://lillehammerartmuseum.com)

49. Take in the Unique Red Sands of Mjelle Beach

If you are a beach lover, forget the overpopulated beach destinations in Spain and Italy and head to Norway for a beach adventure instead. Mjelle beach is one of the most uniquely beautiful beaches that we have ever seen, and the reason for this beauty is its red sand. There is no clear explanation for the gorgeous red sand, so don't ask questions, just enjoy it with a cold drink in your hand, and the sunshine beating down on you.

50. Take in Some Live Music at Bla

Watching some live music in an intimate venue is never going to be a bad idea, and if you are somebody that loves to take in live performances, be sure to check out an Oslo venue that goes by the name of Bla. You can find all kinds of music performances here from the smooth sounds of jazz through to raucous rock bands and epic hip-hop battles. Live performances tend to be in the early evening and then the place transforms into a dance club.

(Brenneriveien 9c, 0182 Oslo; www.blaaoslo.no)

51. Visit Bogstad Manor and Farm

To get a sense of grand old Oslo in years gone by, Bogstad Manor and Farm is the perfect place to visit. This ornate manor house from the 18th century is still furnished with items from the period, so stepping through the manor doors is very much like stepping back in time. If you are travelling with kids, they will fall in love with all the farm animals, which include pigs, goats, cows, sheep, rabbits, and chickens.

(Sørkedalen 450, 0758 Oslo; https://bogstad.no)

52. Hike to the Top of Langfoss Waterfall

Are you a nature lover through and through? Well, you'll be glad to know that Norway is bursting full with nature, and has quite a few spectacular waterfalls. Langfoss waterfall in south Norway is definitely one of the most beautiful. This is the fifth tallest waterfall in the country, and there is a lovely country hike that will take you there. Along the way you will find a picnic area, a summer pasture farm, and eventually the beautiful waterfall itself.

53. Take a Stroll Through Ibsen's Apartment

Henrik Ibsen is one of the most famous and beloved people to ever emerge from Norwegian culture, and it's with good reason. The playwright was hugely influential in the 19th century, and the historic course of theatre plays would look very different without his influence. If you want to know more about the man and his work then be sure to visit Oslo's Ibsen Museum, which is located in the man's refurbished home. Walk around and you'll get to see the original fixtures, furniture, and décor, and really immerse yourself in the world of Ibsen.

(Henrik Ibsens gate 26, 0255 Oslo; https://ibsenmuseet.no/en)

54. Eat a Decadent Meal at a 3 Michelin Star Restaurant

It's no secret that Oslo is a pretty darn expensive city, but if you can't totally splurge now and then is life really worth living at all? And what better way to splurge than by making a reservation at a 3 star Michelin restaurant in the Norwegian capital? Maaemo is the place to chow down on traditional Scandinavian flavours but very elevated. Think a tartlet with a creamy fennel emulsion, a sorbet with freshwater whitefish roe, and a wine list with more than 350 wines to choose from.

(Schweigaards gate 15B, 0191 Oslo; https://maaemo.no)

55. Learn About Norway's Origins at Nordvegen History Centre

These days the most powerful place in Norway is Oslo, its capital city, but that was not always the case. In fact, the small village of Avaldsnes was an ancient power and a really important site of cultural history, and you can find out all about it at the Nordvegen History Centre. You'll learn all about the sovereigns that ruled Norway from this isolated place on the coast, and even get a taste of the magic that people used to believe in thousands of years ago.

(Kong Augvalds veg 103, 4262 Avaldsnes; http://avaldsnes.info/historiesenter)

56. Take in a View of Alesund from Aksla Viewpoint

Alesund is an absolutely stunning fjord city set on the west coast of the country, and it packs in loads of nature with heaps of charm. One thing not to miss there is the ascent from the Aksla viewpoint. There are three ways that you can get to the top of the four hundred and something steps. You can walk, drive, and there's a train that can take you as well. At the top you'll have a view of the whole archipelago. You'll also see the Sunnmore Alps in the background.

57. Spot the Wildlife in Runde

There are lots of little islands off the west coast of Norway, nand visiting these will really give you the opportunity to get away from it all. Runde is a particularly great island for lovers of nature and wildlife – in fact, it has been called Bird Island. While only 150 people live on the island, more than 500,000 seabirds can be found there from February to August. Incredible highlights include puffins, great skuas, gannets, and shags.

58. Visit a Viking Church

Norway is not all pickled herring and stark landscapes, but there is wonderful history to be explored, particularly the Viking history of the country. Urnes Stave Church is a 12th century church that you will find in the beautiful Sognefjord area. As you walk around the church you'll be mesmerised by the weighty sense of history inside the building, and it's still a functioning church today. It was added to the World Heritage List in 1980.

(6870 Ornes; www.stavechurch.com/urnes-stavkirke)

59. Watch a Music Performance at Parkteatrat

If you are in Oslo and stuck for something to do, you can bet your bottom dollar that something will be going on in Parkteatret. This was originally constructed in 1907 as the city's oldest cinema, but these days it is a multimedia venue that is particular popular for live music performances. It also has a separate bar area so if you are simply in search for a cool place to hang out and have a few beers, this ticks the boxes.

(Olaf Ryes plass 11, 0552 Oslo; https://parkteatret.no)

60. Get Close to Sea Life at The Atlantic Sea Park

Norway is a country with huge expanses of water around it, and inside that water is all kinds of wonderful sea life. If you love the idea of exploring the oceans but don't want to get your hair wet, a trip to the Atlantic Sea Park in Alesund could be right up your alley. This is actually one of the most impressive aquariums in Europe, even if you've never heard of Alesund before. Check out the feeding of the seals, pick up a starfish in your hands, and watch the penguins waddle in the Penguin Park.

(6006 Ålesund; http://atlanterhavsparken.no)

61. Visit the World's Strongest Whirlpool in Bodo

Bodo, right in the north of Norway, is a place that many tourists don't end up visiting on their trip to Norway, but you should definitely make the effort if only because it is home to the world's strongest whirlpool. An absolutely ginormous vortex is created because 400 million cubic tonnes of water are pushed through a 3 km long, 150 metre wide strait, and the effect is a whole lot of pressure. It truly is something to behold.

62. Eat a Hearty Lunch of Fiskeboller

The hard truth is that visiting Norway will invariably involve some chilly days. Be sure to bring your best warm clothes with you, but another great way of warming up is to tuck into a hearty meal of fiskeboller. Fiskeboller very simply translates to fish balls, and that's exactly what they are. These fish nuggets are typically served up with potatoes and white sauce. It's filling, warm, and totally delicious.

63. Spend the Night in the Sorrisniva Igloo Hotel

As you travel around Norway, you will probably book a range of hostels, hotels, and guesthouses. There is plenty of very adequate accommodation all around Norway, but why not make your accommodation an event rather than just somewhere to rest your head? Well, an event you will most certainly get at the Sorrisniva Igloo Hotel. The whole place is made of ice and snow, and this is actually the northernmost ice hotel in the world.

(Sorrisniva 20, 9518 Alta; https://sorrisniva.no/)

64. Visit Norway's Oldest Cathedral, Stavanger Cathedral

Norway has stunning landscapes and a local sense of "cool", but history buffs don't get to miss out on the fun because this country also has many impressive historic sites to visit, and where better to start than the oldest cathedral in the whole country, Stavanger Cathedral? The origins of the cathedral dates back to 1125, and while there are original features, it has been renovated over time. It's still in use, so why not pop in for a service?

(Haakon VIIs gate 2, 4600 Stavanger; http://domkirkenogpetri.no)

65. Listen to Smooth Sounds at the Molde Jazz Festival

When you think of places around the world where you're likely to go to a jazz festival, perhaps New Orleans or Paris would spring to mind, but the town of Molde in Norway? It's likely that you haven't even heard of it, and yet this charming town hosts one of the oldest and most celebrated jazz festivals in Europe. It has been taking place every year in July since 1961, and attracts jazz talent from Norway and around the world.

(www.moldejazz.no/en)

66. Visit the Royal Palace in Oslo

As you wander around the city of Oslo, there are a few buildings that deserve that bit more of your attention, and the Royal Palace is one of them. The palace was built in the mid 19th century and is still home to the Norwegian Royal family today. The architecture is impressive with beautiful stuccoed brick, and the park surrounding the building offers wonderful serenity. Be sure to watch the changing of the guards at 1:30pm each day, and take a guided tour if you are really interested.

(Slottsplassen 1, 0010 Oslo)

67. Pass an Artsy Morning at Astrup Fearnley Museet

If you think of art cities around the world, you would almost certainly think of the likes of Paris or Florence before Oslo, but the Norwegian capital has a great assortment of galleries, and one of the most impressive is the Astrup Fearnley Museum of Modern Art. The museum only dates to the early 90s, but has already developed a reputation for quality on the international arts scene, showcasing the works of important artists such as Jeff Koons, Richard Prince, and Cindy Sherman.

(Strandpromenaden 2, 0252 Oslo; http://afmuseet.no/en/hjem)

68. Take a King Crab Safari on the Lang Fjord

When people visit Norway, a lot of them manage to get to Oslo, but the north of the country is far less visited, and it's a wonderful place to get off the beaten track and have some incredible local experiences. If you can find your way to the Lang Fjord, a King Crab safari is an absolute must-do. You will be taken across the thick frozen ice on a snowmobile and your crabbing bucket will be plunged into the deep water to carry up some absolutely gigantic crabs that are perfect for dinner.

69. Start Your Day With a Coffee From Tim Wendelboe

If you are the type of person who cannot start the day without a strong caffeine injection, fear not, because Norwegians are positively coffee obsessed, and you'll find incredible coffee wherever you are in the country. In Oslo, the choice can actually be somewhat overwhelming, and so we'd like to take the liberty of recommending our favourite coffee haunt there: Tim Wendelboe. This coffee shop has its own on-site micro-roastery, and the owner was once named World Barista Champion.

(Grüners gate 1, 0552 Oslo; www.timwendelboe.no)

70. Take the Troll Car Ride to Briksdal Glacier

Norway has a lot of unique landscapes that you just can't find in other places, and during your time in Norway you absolutely have to visit a stunning glacier. The Briksdal Glacier is particularly stunning and the best way to reach it is on a troll car ride. The trip takes you about one and a half hours and will take you through stunning landscapes. Once you arrive, you will be mesmerised by the icy view of the valley below.

71. Explore Local History at Maihaugen

Lillehammer in Norway is probably best known for the Netflix series of the same name, but if you find yourself there you can't miss the opportunity to visit a great museum that goes by the name of Maihaugen. With around 200 buildings, this is actually one of the largest open-air museums in northern Europe. The museum will take you through the history of life in Lillehammer from the 15th century to the present day. Highlights include a school, a prison, a railway station, and a church.

(Maihaugvegen 1, 2609 Lillehammer; https://maihaugen.no)

72. Cycle Through the Morkrid Valley to Drivande Waterfall

Norway offers plenty of opportunities to not just see beautiful things, but to truly immerse yourself in the incomparable landscapes of northern Europe. One of our favourite activities is to cycle along the Morkrid Valley. The biking trip only lasts for about one hour and is pretty manageable for all fitness levels. At the end you'll arrive at the spectacular Drivande waterfall, where you can take a dip and relax after your ride.

73. See Bears and Wolves at Polar Park

Norway is home to many Arctic creatures that are difficult to see in other places. But if you pay a visit to Polar Park in Bardu in northern Norway you can get close to all those magical creatures like sea bears and wolves. This is the northernmost animal park in the whole world, so it's a real one of a kind. A guided tour is included in the ticket price so you really get the chance to understand the lives of the beautiful animals from the park staff.

(Bonesveien 319, 9360 Bardu; http://polarpark.no/Hjem)

74. Take the Kids to the Natural History Museum

Travelling with kids is a double edged sword. On the one hand, it's a real privilege to be able to travel with your kids and create memories that they'll treasure for years to come. But travelling with kids is also challenging for the simple fact that you need to keep them entertained at all times. Something that is both educational and entertaining for kids is the Natural History Museum in Oslo. The zoological part of the museum is very impressive with displays including scenes of arctic wildlife and even a lifesize replica of a beaver dam.

(Sars' gate 1, 0562 Oslo; www.nhm.uio.no/english)

75. Take in the Splendour of Nidaros Cathedral in Trondheim

Norway is typically a destination that attracts more nature lovers than history buffs, but there really are a lot of col historic buildings to check out too, and we are in love with Nidaros Cathedral. Located in Trondheim, this is the northernmost cathedral in the world. It was built all the way back in 1070, and over the tomb of the Viking who bought Christianity to Norway. Climbing to the top will make you short of breath, but it's well worth it.

(Bispegata 11, 7012 Trondheim; www.nidarosdomen.no)

76. Get to Grips With Musical History at Ringve Museum

If you're a music buff, Norway might not seem like the immediate travel destination, but the Ringve Museum shows how music is so important to the core of the Norwegian identity. In this museum, you can find more then 2000 musical instruments on display. There's also a digital archive so you can listen to plenty of music there. If the weather does happen to be good, there is also a beautiful garden on-site.

(Lade alle 60, 7041 Trondheim; https://ringve.no)

77. Tuck Into Cloudberry Desserts at Engebret Café in Oslo

Travelling is fun, but every now and then you just want to take a break, sit down in a charming café, and have a coffee with a lovely dessert. Fortunately, the city of Oslo is positively teeming with cafes, but one that really stands out for us is Engebret Café. This café has roots that date way back to 1857 so they really know what they are doing. Do not miss the selection of cloudberry desserts on the menu. If you've not tried cloudberries before, they are quite sour, but somehow very creamy at the same time. Definitely something to taste.

(1 Bankplassen, 0151 Oslo; www.engebret-cafe.no)

78. Rummage Around the Bryggerekka Flea Market

Norway has a reputation of being a pretty expensive place to travel, and that is true to a certain extent. But there is always a way to do things on a budget, and it's totally possible to shop til you drop and find some fantastic deals at the Bryggerekka Flea Market in Trondheim. This particular market is mainly filled with antiques, and you can also find vintage clothing dotted around. Oh, and there are regular stops for coffee and waffles through the market too.

(Kongens gate 2, 7011 Trondheim)

79. Sip on a Glass of Wine or Two at Territoriet

There are certain times when a perfect evening consists of nothing more than kicking back with a great glass of wine, and when that moment strikes, you just need to head to Territoriet in Oslo, quite possibly the loveliest wine bar in the city. There are more than 300 wines available by the glass so there is something for everyone whether you're into fruity reds, dry whites, or anything in between.

(Markveien 58, 0550 Oslo; www.territoriet.no)

80. Hunt for Treasures at the Birkelunden Bric-A-Brac Market

If you are something of a shopaholic, Oslo is definitely the place where you'll be able to easily empty your wallet. But actually, you don't need to bankrupt yourself to purchase some really cool things in the Norwegian capital city. The Birkelunden Bric-A-Brac market is the place to find used items that extend right back to the 1940s. Whether you are shopping for furniture, vinyl records, or clothes, you can find something for you. The market is open most Sundays.

81. Be Mesmerised by the Power of Steinsdalsfossen Waterfall

There are some things in life that are universally pleasing, and standing in front of a gushing waterfall on a bright and sunny day is something that everybody would love. If you can't get enough of waterfalls, the Steinsdalsfossen waterfall is an attraction you certainly will not want to miss. The waterfall gushes down 50 metres, and the really impressive thing about this waterfall is that you can walk behind it and remain bone dry.

(Mo ved Steinsdalen, 5600 Norheimsund)

82. Take in the Grandeur of Oslo Cathedral

One of the absolute must-visit buildings in the Norwegian capital is Oslo Cathedral. Dating all the way back to the 17th century, this church has some of the most beautifully elaborate stained glass windows that we have ever seen, and the painted ceiling is just as ornate. It is totally free to enter at any time, so take your time and enjoy the flood of peace and tangible sense of history as you sit in the pews. *(Karl Johans gate 11, 0154 Oslo)*

83. Enjoy a Spot of Sunbathing on Godalen Beach

When you think of beautiful beach destinations in Europe, you would no doubt think of the Mediterranean or Adriatic seas first, but do not forget that Norway has lots of water around it, and coastline equals beaches. One of the most charming beaches in Norway is Godalen beach. On sunny days, when the Norwegian days last for almost 24 hours, this is the perfect spot for sunbathing. There's also designated spots for barbecues, and a play area for children.

84. Sip on Local Craft Beer at Aegir Brewpub

One of the great benefits of travelling destinations is that you get to try out new things, and if you are a beer lover, you will certainly want to try some of the local Norwegian beers that haven't reached foreign shores. Fortunately, the craft beer movement is also burgeoning in Norway, and the Aegir Brewpub in Flam is a wonderful place to sink a few glasses. The actual place is just as impressive as the beer. It's inspired by Norse mythology and has the feeling of a stave church.

(A-Feltvegen 23, 5743 Flåm)

85. Get to Grips With Skiing at the Holmenkollen Ski Museum

If you can't get enough of winter sports, Norway is 100% the country for you. Of course, there are many places where you can hit the slopes across the country, but if you are truly ski obsessed, a couple of hours at the Holmenkollen Ski Museum wouldn't go amiss either. The museum was founded back in 1923, and this makes it the world's oldest ski museum. Visit and you'll be taken on a journey of 4000 years of ski history, even getting to see ancient stone carvings relating to skiing.

(Kongeveien 5, 0787 Oslo; www.skiforeningen.no/holmenkollen)

86. Take a Walk Along Trolltunga Cliff

Norway is a country with no shortage of epic views of its stunning scenery, and if you want a few Instagram-able moments, you really can't get more beautiful than the view from Trolltunga cliff. A warning: the hike to this viewpoint is not for the faint hearted. It will take you around ten to twelve hours, and it's tough along the way. You'll reach an elevation of 1100 metres, and the views are nothing short of breath taking. This hike is only possible from June to September.

87. Shop for Second Hand Treasures at Fretex

Sopping til you drop might just render you bankrupt in Norway, but there is one store that offers all kinds of goodies at very competitive prices. Fretex is a brand that has over 50 stores across Norway that sell second-hand goods. Rummage through their shops and you will find vintage clothing, cool old jewellery, used books, ornaments for the home, and pretty much everything in between.

(www.fretex.no)

88. Try Cross Country Skiing in Rondane National Park

There are so many ways to get active in the outdoors in Norway, and an adventure with cross country skiing is certainly one of the most adventurous. There seems to be endless space in Norway so there is plenty of opportunity for this, but Rondane National Park is one of the best destinations. Located in the centre of the country, this is Norway's oldest national park with ten mountain peaks. If you visit in the summer skip the skiing and try swimming instead.

(www.nasjonaleturistveger.no/en/routes/rondane)

89. Spend a Night in the Trees at Engerdal

There are plenty of very lovely hotels strewn across Norway, but why not make your accommodation an experience in its own right rather than just somewhere to catch up on sleep? That's exactly what you can do at Kraggbua in Engerdal. The cool thing about this place is that it has tree cabins nestled 7 metres above the ground in the treetops. You'll go to sleep and wake up to the sound of leaves rustling and chirping birds.

(Granbergveien 727, Engerdal)

90. Party Hard at PUNKT Festival

While it's true that summer music festivals in Norway are not well known the world over, this is not to say that there are not some epic festivals to be enjoyed. If you are into edgy electronic music, the annual PUNKT festival in Kristiansand is truly not to be missed. The festival has been running since 2005 and typically takes place at the end of August each year. With local and international talent taking over the decks, hardcore dance fans should not miss this one.

(http://punktfestival.no)

91. Go Island Hopping in the Sognefjord

Norway is a pretty big country, but it's not only the mainland that you should be exploring on your trip, because actually there's an absolutely huge number of islands off the coast. For getting away from it all and enjoying some really unique and beautiful landscapes, don't miss a collection of small islands called Sognefjord. Hire a kayak and take in the views.

92. Take in the Blooms in Oslo's University Botanic Garden

If you are a nature lover, there is plenty to explore all around Norway, but while in Oslo one of the best places you can visit is the botanical garden of Oslo University. The garden dates all the way back to the mid 19th century and covers an area of 150,000 square metres, i.e. it's absolutely huge. There's more than 1800 different plant species to be explored, and you'll have the opportunity to wander a scent garden with beautifully perfumed flowers, a palm house with extravagant palms, and more besides.

(Sars' gate 1, 0562 Oslo)

93. Indulge an Arts Lover at the Annual Mela Festival

If you love everything about the arts, you might think of going to a city like London or Paris before you make the trip to Norway, but arts lovers are sure to have a great time at the annual Mela Festival. The free festival typically takes place in Oslo over about three days in the middle of August. It is hosted on the picturesque harbour, and you can catch free music concerts, dance performances, stalls selling original artwork, craft, and jewellery, and tonnes more fun besides.

(www.mela.no)

94. Learn Something New at the Trondelag Folk Museum

It's a good idea to have some museum ideas up your sleeve, and one museum you won't want to miss in Trondheim is the Trondelag Folk Museum. This open air museum is located around the ruins of King Sverre's castle. You will experience life in Trondheim from the 18th century to today as you walk through the various buildings and outdoor farm spaces.

(Sverresborg Alle 13, 7020 Trondheim; https://sverresborg.no)

95. Watch an Independent Film at Cinemateket

Travelling to new places offers wonderful and unforgettable experiences, but it can also be exhausting, and there are times when all you have the energy for is kicking back and watching a fantastic film. When that moment strikes, Cinemateket is the number one place to go. We love this movie theatre because they are committed to showing classic and obscure movies outside of the mainstream blockbusters. Many films are imported just to be shown at this one cinema.

(Dronningens gate 16, 0105 Oslo; www.cinemateket.no)

96. Play a Game of Shuffleboard at Kulturhuset

Kulturhuset, literally meaning Culture House, is a veritable treasure trove of experiences and activities in the heart of Oslo. You can find exhibitions, debates, and concerts, but what we really love about this place is its dedication to shuffleboard. Upstairs you can play the game with friends, and if you are travelling alone, it's a great place to actually make some new friends over a fun activity.

(Youngs gate 6, 0181 Oslo; http://kulturhusetioslo.no)

97. Enjoy a World of Dance at Oktoberdans

If you are a dance fanatic or you just fancy catching a few cool dance performances, make sure your trip coincides with Oktoberdans, which is Norway's only international dance festival. As the name suggests, the festival is hosted in October, and it showcases many dance performances that really push the art form of dance. Don't expect classic ballet performances as this is the place to see dance right on the cutting edge.

(http://bit-teatergarasjen.no/festivaler/oktoberdans-2018)

98. Feel Festive at the Roros Christmas Market

One of the most wonderful things about travelling through Europe during the winter months are the incredible Christmas markets. With its blankets of snow, where better to feel festive than Norway? And boy will you feel festive when you find your way to the Roros Christmas Market in a picturesque part of the centre of the country. The market only opens for one weekend, but it's worth planning to attend. You'll hear carols being sung by school kids, you can see Santa's reindeer, chow down on freshly baked gingerbread, and lots more fun besides.

99. Hit a Few Balls at the Bjaavann Golf Club

A great holiday means different things to different people. While some love epic adventures or strolling around museums, there are others who are very happy to pack their golf clubs and spend endless days on the golfing green. If that sounds like you, you have many courses to choose from across Norway, and Bjaavann Golf Club might just be the very best of them all. The course has parts with tall grass, a winding river, and even a lake.

(Østre Ålefjærvei 195, 4634 Kristiansand S; https://bjaavanngk.no)

100. Go Sea Kayaking off the Coast of Tromso

The coastline of Norway is absolutely gorgeous, and it is worth braving the chill of the Atlantic ocean to explore this gorgeous part of the country. Tromso is a very beautiful place with astounding coastline. Of course, you can take walks along the coast, but it's even better to get right into the ocean and enjoy some fun sea kayaking. You'll get to see the gorgeous blue water beneath you, and the stunning mountain scenery on the coast.

101. Visit Njardarheimr Viking Village

Viking history is an important part of Norway's cultural identity, and a trip to the Njardarheimr Viking Village will immerse you in this culture. This is a built authentic village that represents how the Vikings lived 1000 years ago. You will have the chance to try axe throwing, archery, you can chat with the Vikings, and see how they make their handicrafts. This is the best place to get kids interested in history without dragging them around a regular museum against their will.

(www.vikingvalley.no)

Before You Go…

Thanks for reading **101 Amazing Things to Do in Norway.** We hope that it makes your trip a memorable one!

Have a wonderful time, and don't eat too much pickled herring!

Team 101 Amazing Things

Printed in the USA
CPSIA information can be obtained
at www.ICGtesting.com
LVHW091631190724
785881LV00005B/722